I0483152

Guidelines for Employers to Reduce Motor Vehicle Crashes

This document represents a joint effort by NETS, NHTSA and OSHA to reduce motor vehicle-related deaths and injuries in the nation's workforce.

This [white paper] was funded under [Purchase Order Number B-9-4-2-3576] for the U.S. Department of Labor, Occupational Safety and Health Administration. The views expressed herein do not necessarily represent the official position or policy of the U.S. Department of Labor.

Every 12 minutes someone dies in a motor vehicle crash, every 10 seconds an injury occurs and every 5 seconds a crash occurs. Many of these incidents occur during the workday or during the commute to and from work. Employers bear the cost for injuries that occur both on and off the job. Whether you manage a fleet of vehicles, oversee a mobile sales force or simply employ commuters, by implementing a driver safety program in the workplace you can greatly reduce the risks faced by your employees and their families while protecting your company's bottom line.

Set Up a Safe Driving Program to Keep Your Employees Safe on the Road

Motor vehicle crashes are a leading cause of death and injury for all ages. Crashes on and off the job have far-reaching financial and psychological effects on employees, their co-workers and families, and their employers.

You need a driver safety program:

- To save lives and to reduce the risk of life-altering injuries within your workforce.
- To protect your organization's human and financial resources.
- To guard against potential company and personal liabilities associated with crashes involving employees driving on company business.

Your program should work to keep the driver and those with whom he/she shares the road safe. And, if necessary, the program must work to change driver attitudes, improve behavior, and increase skills to build a "be safe" culture. By instructing your employees in basic safe driving practices and then rewarding safety-conscious behavior, you can help your employees and their families avoid tragedy.

Employees are an employer's most valuable assets. Workplace driver safety programs not only make good business sense but also are a good employee relations tool, demonstrating that employers care about their employees.

This booklet outlines ten steps for building a driver safety program in your workplace. These steps will be useful to any organization regardless of size of the organization, type of traffic encountered, number of vehicles involved, or whether employees drive company or personal vehicles for work purposes. Also included are real-life examples of successful safety programs, key traffic safety issues to address in the workplace, instructions for calculating your organization's loss from motor vehicle crashes, and a list of resources to help you fine-tune your program.

Promoting Safe Driving Practices Helps Your Bottom Line

Motor vehicle crashes cost employers $60 billion annually in medical care, legal expenses, property damage, and lost productivity. They drive up the cost of benefits such as workers' compensation, Social Security, and private health and disability insurance. In addition, they increase the company overhead involved in administering these programs.

The average crash costs an employer $16,500. When a worker has an on-the-job crash that results in an injury, the cost to their employer is $74,000. Costs can exceed $500,000 when a fatality is involved. Off-the-job crashes are costly to employers as well.[1]

The real tragedy is that these crashes are largely preventable. Recognizing the opportunity that employers have to save lives, a growing number of employers have established traffic safety programs in their companies. No organization can afford to ignore a major problem that has such a serious impact on both their personnel and the company budget.

[1] *NHTSA [2003]. The economic burden of traffic crashes on employers: costs by state and industry and by alcohol and restraint use. Publication DOT HS 809 682.*

Calculate Your Costs for Motor Vehicle Crashes

To understand the impact of motor vehicle crashes on your organization, use the Costs of Traffic Crashes to Employers Worksheet, found at the end of this booklet, to calculate the cost of your crashes. You may want to initially select one recent crash to illustrate the magnitude and complexity of such losses. Once you master the worksheet for one crash, you can then apply it to all the crashes experienced in a chosen time frame (e.g., annually) within your organization to characterize your crash loss profile.

Once you know the costs associated with motor vehicle crashes you will realize that the costs associated with implementing a driver safety program are minimal compared to the costs of crashes to your organization. Examples abound of the positive return-on-investment (ROI) realized by companies – small, medium, and large – that have implemented well-designed safety programs for the benefit of their employees. In fact, the Liberty Mutual Insurance Company reported in 2001 that, based on its Executive Survey of Workplace Safety, 61 percent of surveyed business executives believe their companies receive an ROI of $3.00 or more for every $1.00 they spent on improving workplace safety.[2]

[2] *Liberty Mutual Insurance Company [2001]. Liberty Mutual Executive Survey of Workplace Safety.*

Where to Start

Depending on the size of your organization, you may have access to all of the data that you need. Or you may need to work with your human resource manager, safety manager, workers' compensation representative, accountants, and medical and motor vehicle insurance representatives to obtain the numbers you'll need.

Costs of Motor Vehicle Crashes to Employers Worksheet
Use the worksheet found at the end of this booklet to estimate the cost of a motor vehicle crash to your organization. The costs included on the worksheet will be estimates based upon the records, receipts and recall of those involved with the crash. It may be helpful to consult copies of accident reports, police reports, damage receipts, insurance claim records and payroll records. It is often very difficult to identify all costs associated with these crashes, so use the best information you have available. If your company incurred expenses not listed on the worksheet, be sure to include them.

Many companies have already benefited from the approach to driver safety outlined in this booklet. Here's how:

Nationwide Insurance - Columbus, Ohio

Program:

- Nationwide, one of the largest insurance and financial services companies in the United States, operates a large, private motor vehicle fleet.
- In 1998, Nationwide developed and implemented a comprehensive motor vehicle safety program using a 10-step program as outlined in this booklet.

Results:

- While the number of miles driven by Nationwide associates has increased by 19 percent, the organization's preventable crashes have decreased by 53 percent.
- The organization's total motor vehicle loss costs are down 40 percent.

Charter Communications – Michigan

Program:

- Charter Communications provides cable service to Michigan residents. With a fleet of over 650 vehicles, Charter employees drive 1.5 million miles per month.
- In early 2001, the company began a program to increase seat belt use among their company drivers. Charter worked with Michigan NETS to establish a corporate seat belt program and to reward seat belt use.
- Participation in the NETS annual Drive Safely Work Week campaign and the NHTSA "Safety Belt Award Program" were both used to support the corporate program.
- During this same period, Charter began a defensive driving program for employees.

Results:

- In 2001, Charter-Michigan Region's seat belt use rate was 74 percent. In two years, they reached a 94 percent seat belt use rate and have continued to maintain that rate.

- They also experienced a 30 percent decrease in motor vehicle crashes during this time.

General Motors Corporation - Detroit, Michigan
Program:
- GM, the world's largest vehicle manufacturer, implemented the Safe Driving Program, "Create the Habit," for over 250,000 employees in November 1998.
- This comprehensive initiative provided workplace education programs and strict seat belt usage policies.
- An incentive program was developed to recognize and reward seat belt use. GM surveyed 90 sites each quarter.

Results:
- GM increased employee seat belt usage from 61 percent in 1998 to 85 percent by December 2003. Ongoing awareness programs continue to promote the safety message.
- The Safe Driving Program is credited with saving five lives a year.

Pike Industries - Barre, Vermont
Program:
- Pike Industries, an asphalt paving company, has approximately 250 employees in Vermont. They operate the 280 vehicles (pickups, tractor-trailers, dump trucks, etc.) in the fleet.
- Their fleet safety program requires all new drivers to receive classroom training; each is assigned a veteran "mentor." Veteran drivers attend annual classroom training, reviewing topics that include federal regulations and accident avoidance techniques.
- All drivers attend weekly "toolbox" talks to discuss fleet safety topics.

Results:
- Company drivers traveled over 2 million miles in 2003 hauling construction equipment and materials, performing construction activities (many were in highly dangerous work zones) and did not have any significant roadway incidents.
- Workers' compensation claims for vehicle incidents dropped from a high of 73 percent of total losses in 2001 to 2 percent in 2003. Vehicle property damage losses also followed this trend.

NETS 10-Step Program to Minimize Crash Risk

The 10-Step Program provides guidelines for what an employer can do to improve traffic safety performance and minimize the risk of motor vehicle crashes. Following these steps helps to ensure that you hire capable drivers, only allow eligible drivers to drive on company business, train them, supervise them, and maintain company vehicles properly. Adherence to these 10 steps can also help to keep your motor vehicle insurance costs as low as possible.

1. Senior Management Commitment & Employee Involvement
2. Written Policies and Procedures
3. Driver Agreements
4. Motor Vehicle Record (MVR) Checks
5. Crash Reporting and Investigation
6. Vehicle Selection, Maintenance and Inspection
7. Disciplinary Action System
8. Reward/Incentive Program
9. Driver Training/Communication
10. Regulatory Compliance

These steps are from the NETS *Traffic Safety Primer: A Guidebook for Employers.*

Step 1: Senior Management Commitment and Employee Involvement

The safety of an organization's employees as they drive for work and to and from work is so important that it requires the attention of top-level management. Senior management can provide leadership, set policies, and allocate resources (staff and budget) to create a safety culture. Actively encouraging employee participation and involvement at all levels of the organization is a good practice and will help the effort to succeed. Workers and their representatives must be involved in the initial planning phase.

Step 2: Written Policies and Procedures

A written statement emphasizing the commitment to reducing traffic-related deaths and injuries is essential to a successful program. Create a clear, comprehensive and enforceable set of traffic safety policies and communicate them to all employees. These are the cornerstones of an effective driver safety program. Post them throughout the workplace, distribute copies periodically, and discuss the policies at company meetings. Offer incentives for sticking to the rules, and point out the consequences of disregarding them. Below are sample policies that can be adapted for use by your company.

Sample Alcohol and Drug Use Policy
(Name of Company/Organization) has a vital interest in maintaining safe, healthy, and efficient working conditions for its employees. Therefore, the consumption of alcohol or illegal drugs by any employee during "duty hours" is prohibited. Duty hours consist of all working hours, including break periods and on-call periods, whether on or off company premises. The consumption of alcohol or illegal drugs while performing company business or while in a company facility is prohibited.

Sample Seat Belt Use Policy

(Name of Company/Organization) recognizes that seat belts are extremely effective in preventing injuries and loss of life. It is a simple fact that wearing your seat belt can reduce your risk of dying in a traffic crash by 45 percent in a car and by as much as 60 percent in a truck or SUV.

We care about our employees, and want to make sure that no one is injured or killed in a tragedy that could have been prevented by the use of seat belts. Therefore, all employees of (Name of Company/Organization) must wear seat belts when operating a company-owned vehicle, or any vehicle on company premises or on company business; and all occupants are to wear seat belts or, where appropriate, child restraints when riding in a company-owned vehicle, or in a personal vehicle being used for company business. All employees and their families are strongly encouraged to always use seat belts and the proper child restraints whenever they are driving or riding in any vehicle, in any seating position.

Step 3: Driver Agreements

Establish a contract with all employees who drive for work purposes, whether they drive assigned company vehicles or drive their personal vehicles. By signing an agreement, the driver acknowledges awareness and understanding of the organization's traffic safety policies, procedures, and expectations regarding driver performance, vehicle maintenance and reporting of moving violations.

Step 4: Motor Vehicle Record (MVR) Checks

Check the driving records of all employees who drive for work purposes. You must screen out drivers who have poor driving records since they are most likely to cause problems in the future. The MVR should be reviewed periodically to ensure that the driver maintains a good driving record. Clearly define the number of violations an employee/driver can have before losing the privilege of driving for work, and provide training where indicated.

Step 5: Crash Reporting and Investigation

Establish and enforce a crash reporting and investigation pro-cess. All crashes, regardless of severity, should be reported to the employee's supervisor as soon as feasible after the incident. Company traffic safety policies and procedures should clearly guide drivers through their responsibilities in a crash situation. All crashes should be reviewed to determine their cause and whether or not the incidents were preventable. Understanding the root causes of crashes and why they are happening, regardless of fault, forms the basis for eliminating them in the future.

Step 6: Vehicle Selection, Maintenance and Inspection
Selecting, properly maintaining and routinely inspecting company vehicles is an important part of preventing crashes and related losses.

It is advisable that the organization review and consider the safety features of all vehicles to be considered for use. Those vehicles that demonstrate "best in class" status for crash-worthiness and overall safety should be chosen and made available to drivers.

For the latest information on crash test ratings and other important vehicle safety information, visit www.safercar.gov. To report a concern about a defect or problem with your vehicle, contact the NHTSA Auto Safety Hotline at: 1-888-DASH-2-DOT.

Vehicles should be on a routine preventive maintenance schedule for servicing and checking of safety-related equip-ment. Regular maintenance should be done at specific mileage intervals consistent with the manufacturer's recom-mendations. A mechanic should do a thorough inspection of each vehicle at least annually with documented results placed in the vehicle's file.

Personal vehicles used for company business are not necessarily subject to the same criteria and are generally the responsibility of the owner. However, personal vehicles used on company business should be maintained in a manner that provides the employee with maximum safety and reflects positively on the company.

Step 7: Disciplinary Action System

Develop a strategy to determine the course of action after the occurrence of a moving violation and/or "preventable" crash. There are a variety of corrective action programs available; the majority of these are based on a system that assigns points for moving violations. The system should provide for progressive discipline if a driver begins to develop a pattern of repeated traffic violations and/or preventable crashes. The system should describe what specific action(s) will be taken if a driver accumulates a certain number of violations or preventable crashes in any pre-defined period.

Step 8: Reward/Incentive Program

Develop and implement a driver reward/incentive program to make safe driving an integral part of your business culture. Safe driving behaviors contribute directly to the bottom line and should be recognized as such. Positive results are realized when driving performance is incorporated into the overall evaluation of job performance. Reward and incentive programs typically involve recognition, monetary rewards, special privileges or the use of incentives to motivate the achievement of a predetermined goal or to increase participation in a program or event.

Step 9: Driver Training/Communication

Provide continuous driver safety training and communication. Even experienced drivers benefit from periodic training and reminders of safe driving practices and skills. It is easy to become complacent and not think about the consequences of our driving habits.

Step 10: Regulatory Compliance

Ensure adherence to highway safety regulations. It is important to clearly establish which, if any, local, state, and/or federal regulations govern your vehicles and/or drivers. These regulations may involve, but may not necessarily be limited to the:

- Federal Motor Carrier Safety Administration (FMCSA)

- U.S. Department of Transportation (USDOT)

- National Highway Transportation Safety Administration (NHTSA)

- Federal Highway Administration (FHWA)

- Employment Standards Administration (ESA)

The increasing traffic congestion on our nation's roadways wastes significant time and money, reduces productivity and promotes risky driving behavior. Employees may feel pressured to drive faster and for longer periods of time and to engage in potentially distracting in-vehicle activities to meet their job responsibilities. Engaging in unsafe driving practices affects those who occasionally drive their personal vehicles for work purposes as well as those who spend their workday driving a company vehicle.

As an employer, do your part by keeping your parking lot well lighted and well maintained. Keep roadway and parking spaces properly striped, and clear of debris and snow. Install signs at parking lot exits reminding employees to buckle their seat belts and drive safely. Let your concern for their safety be their final thought as they leave your parking lot.

Employers have enormous power to protect their businesses by educating their employees about safe driving practices. The safety issues described below should be addressed in an employee awareness and training program.

More detailed information on Aggressive Driving, Distracted Driving, Drowsy Driving and Impaired Driving can be found beginning on page 27.

Secure Materials for Transport

Tools or equipment should be secured while being transported to prevent unsafe movement of materials. During a crash or when making sudden maneuvers, loose objects can slide around or become airborne, injuring the driver and any passengers. Objects that could become a hazard should be secured or stored outside the passenger compartment.

Seat Belt Use

Seat belts are the single most effective means of reducing deaths and serious injuries in traffic crashes. As the most effective safety device in vehicles, they save nearly 12,000 lives and prevent 325,000 serious injuries in America each year. During a crash, anyone not wearing a seat belt will slam into the steering wheel, windshield, or other parts of the interior, or be ejected from the vehicle.

Distracted Driving

Distracted driving is a factor in 25 to 30 percent of all traffic crashes. With hectic schedules and roadway delays, many employees feel pressured to multi-task just to keep up with their personal and work-related responsibilities. More time on the road means less time at home or at work but "drive time" can never mean "down time." Since drivers make more than 200 decisions during every mile traveled, it's critical for employers to stress that when driving for work, safe driving is their primary responsibility.

Alcohol and Drug Impaired Driving

Alcohol use is involved in 40 percent of all fatal motor vehicle crashes, representing an average of one alcohol-related fatality every 30 minutes. It is estimated that three in every 10 Americans will be involved in an impaired driving-related crash some time in their life. Alcohol, certain prescription drugs, over-the-counter medications, and illegal drugs can all affect a person's ability to drive safely due to decreased alertness, concentration, coordination and reaction time. Busi-nesses pay a high price for alcohol and drug abuse; alcohol is a contributing factor in 39 percent of all work-related traffic crashes.

Fatigued Driving

Fatigued or drowsy driving may be involved in more than 100,000 crashes each year, resulting in 40,000 injuries and 1,550 deaths. Sadly, these numbers represent only the tip of the iceberg since these crashes are seriously under-reported. These days, it's more important than ever for employees to be well rested, alert and sober on the road so that they are in a position to defend themselves from drivers who do not make the same choice. Train employees to make smart decisions when they're behind the wheel, on and off the job.

Aggressive Driving

Employees commuting to and from work and traveling for work purposes often find themselves caught up in bottlenecks and traffic delays, wasting their time and reducing their productivity. These situations create a high level of frustration that can spark aggressive driving behavior. The roadway is one place that being aggressive never pays.

Aggressive driving acts include excessive speed, tailgating, failure to signal a lane change, running a red light and passing on the right. The best advice is to avoid engaging in conflict with other drivers and to allow others to merge.

Young Drivers

The 16-20-year-old population represents a significant highway safety problem. Traffic crashes are the leading cause of fatalities for teens. Historically, this group is the age group that has the lowest seat belt use rate and is the most likely to engage in risky driving behaviors that include: speeding, driving while alcohol or drug impaired and when drowsy. It is important for employers with young workers to actively promote safe driving practices.

We have learned much about teen driver safety during the past decade. There are proven, specific safety benefits from a variety of best practices that are commonly referred to as "graduated driver licensing" or GDL. GDL practices have resulted in substantial reductions in crashes, injuries and fatalities for novice teenage drivers.

Under Federal law, 16-year-old workers are prohibited from driving as part of their job, and 17-year-olds may drive for work only under strictly limited circumstances. Some state laws may be more restrictive than Federal laws. For more information on child labor laws visit, www.youthrules.dol.gov or www.cdc.gov/niosh/topics/youth/.

Reach Out to Family and Community Members

Once your driver safety program is operational, consider extending it to your employees' families and members of your community. Employers are in a position to foster safe driving practices and reduce the number of traffic crashes in their communities. Employer programs not only inform employees about traffic hazards and educate them about responsible driving practices but they can create a safer road-way environment for the entire community.

Four reasons for reaching out to employees' families and members of the community:

- Provides public relations benefits for your company.
- Boosts employee morale.
- Creates a safer driving environment for your employees, their dependents, and members of the community.
- Reduces employer and employee healthcare costs.

Where to Go for Additional Information

For more information and assistance in implementing a traffic safety program in your workplace, you can contact the Network of Employers for Traffic Safety (NETS), the National Highway Traffic Safety Administration (NHTSA), the Occupational Safety and Health Administration (OSHA) or the National Institute for Occupational Safety and Health (NIOSH).

National Highway Traffic Safety Administration
NHTSA's mission is to save lives, prevent injuries, and reduce traffic-related health care and other economic costs. The organization can provide technical assistance, various highway safety awareness materials, and other support for your program. For more information on highway safety programs, visit www.nhtsa.dot.gov or contact NHTSA at 400 Seventh Street, SW, Washington, DC 20590.

National Institute for Occupational Safety and Health
NIOSH, as the national agency responsible for occupational safety and health research, is committed to reducing the toll of work-related roadway crashes on American workers. Prevention of work-related crashes poses one of the greatest challenges in occupational safety. The roadway is a unique environment. Compared with other work settings, employers' ability to control working conditions and to exert direct supervisory controls is limited. Workers may be pressured to drive faster and for longer periods and to use technologies that may lead to inattention to the driving task. The problem of work-related crashes affects those who occasionally drive personal vehicles on the job as well as those who routinely drive commercial motor vehicles over long distances. For more information on motor vehicle occupational research visit: www.cdc.gov/niosh or contact NIOSH at 1-800-35-NIOSH or 1-800-356-4674.

Network of Employers for Traffic Safety

NETS is an employer-led, nonprofit, public/private partnership dedicated to improving the safety and health of employees, their families, and members of the communities in which they live and work, by reducing the number of traffic crashes that occur on and off the job. NETS provides employers of all sizes and industry types with effective programs, policies, best practices, and employer-led activities, whether an employee drives for work or to and from work. Drive Safely Work Week (DSWW) is an annual campaign sponsored by NETS to promote safe driving practices for all employees. For further information on NETS, the 10-Step Program, and DSWW, visit www.trafficsafety.org or contact NETS at 1-800-221-0045.

Occupational Safety and Health Administration

Employers are responsible for providing a safe and healthful workplace for their employees. OSHA's role is to assure the safety and health of America's workers by setting and enforcing standards; providing training, outreach, and education; establishing partnerships; and encouraging continual improvement in workplace safety and health. Information on motor vehicle safety can be found on OSHA's website at www.osha.gov/SLTC/motorvehiclesafety/index.html

The following pages contain more detailed information on Aggressive Driving, Distracted Driving, Drowsy Driving, Impaired Driving and a worksheet, Costs of Motor Vehicle Crashes to Employers.

Aggressive Driving

As traffic congestion continues to grow, motorists commuting to and from work and traveling for business purposes often find themselves caught up in bottlenecks and significant delays, wasting time and reducing their productivity. This situation creates a high level of frustration and can spark aggressive driving among these overwhelmed drivers. To protect against aggressive driving, remember that your primary responsibility is to drive focused and stay safe.

Safety Facts for the Road

- A major reason for increased traffic congestion is that our highway system has not kept pace with the growing demands placed on it. Since 1970, the number of drivers increased by 64% while the roadway system increased by only 6%.
- Many Americans believe aggressive driving is on the rise and worry about the behavior of other drivers but admit to engaging in aggressive driving themselves.
- A substantial number of the 6.8 million crashes that occur each year are estimated to be caused by aggressive driving.
- Overly frustrated drivers are turning their cars into extensions of their homes and offices, creating a dangerous distraction on the road that fuels aggressive driving among other drivers.

Drive Focused. Stay Safe. Avoid Aggressive Driving.

- Correct your own unsafe driving habits that are likely to endanger, antagonize or provoke other drivers.
- Keep your cool in traffic; be patient and courteous to other drivers and don't take their actions personally.
- If you think you have a problem, seek help. Look for anger or stress management classes or self-help books.
- Reduce your stress on the road by allowing plenty of time to reach your destination, plan your route in advance and alter your schedule or route to avoid busy roads.
- If despite all your planning, you're going to arrive late, accept it and avoid aggressive driving.
- Make every attempt to safely move out of an aggressive driver's way. If a hostile motorist tries to pick a fight, do not make eye contact and do not respond. Ignore gestures and refuse to return them.
- Report aggressive driving to the police. Provide a vehicle description, license number, location and the direction of travel.

Are you "just driving like everyone else" or are you driving aggressively?

The Nerves of Steel Survey is a national survey that reveals how Americans define aggressive driving.

Is this act aggressive?

Tailgating	95%
Making rude gestures	91%
Passing on the shoulder	90%
Pulling into parking space someone else is waiting for	88%
Failing to yield to merging traffic	85%
Flashing high beams at the car in front of you	74%
Waiting until the last second to merge with traffic on the highway	66%
Changing lanes without signaling	66%
Driving through a yellow light that is turning red	62%
Honking the horn	53%
Double parking	53%
Driving 10 mph or more under the speed limit	27%

The Steel Alliance, 2002.

For more information on aggressive driving, contact NETS at 1-888-221-0045 or visit: www.trafficsafety.org.

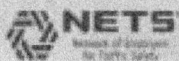

Distracted Driving

Longer commutes, an increase in heavy traffic, the availability of in-vehicle technology are all factors that result in driver distraction. More time in your vehicle results in less time at home or on the job, causing drivers to feel the pressure to multi-task to keep up with their responsibilities. Countless distractions tempt drivers to forget that their primary responsibility is to drive focused and stay safe.

Safety Facts for the Road
- Distracted driving is estimated to be a factor in between 25 to 30% of all traffic crashes—that's 4,000 or more crashes a day.
- Events inside and outside the vehicle can distract a driver. Adverse roadway and weather conditions require a driver's full attention.
- While taking one's eyes off the road presents obvious risks, activities that take a driver's mind away from driving are just as risky.
- A driver's ability to manage distractions varies widely and can change from day-to-day depending on their level of stress and fatigue.
- Distracted drivers fail to recognize potential hazards in the road and react more slowly to traffic conditions, decreasing their "margin of safety."
- Research suggests that distracted driving increases the risk of rear-end and single-vehicle crashes.

Do you know when you're driving distracted?
- Has a passenger in your car screamed or gasped because of something you did or did not do?
- Did you run a stop sign unintentionally?
- Have you slammed on your brakes because you didn't see the car in front of you stop?
- You do not remember driving from one place to another?

Drive Focused. Stay Safe. Avoid Distracted Driving.
- Safe driving practices require that you constantly search the roadway ahead for situations that could require you to take quick action.
- Recognize that driving requires your full attention.

Did you know that even the most routine activities are potentially distracting while driving?

A national survey revealed the activities that distract today's drivers.

NETS DISTRACTED DRIVING SURVEY
Activities Drivers Engage in While Driving

96%	Talking to passengers
89%	Adjusting vehicle climate/radio controls
74%	Eating a meal/snack
51%	Using a cell phone
41%	Tending to children
34%	Reading a map/publication
19%	Grooming
11%	Preparing for work

Participation in Distracting Activities While Driving for Work or for Personal Purposes

57%	Personal purposes
25%	Work purposes
14%	Both equally
2%	Don't drive for work
3%	Don't know

Network of Employers for Traffic Safety, 2001.

For more information on aggressive driving, contact NETS at 1-888-221-0045 or visit: www.trafficsafety.org.

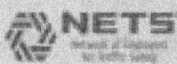 **NETS** Remember, the best defense against aggressive drivers is a seat belt! Buckling up is the single most effective action you can take to protect yourself from serious injury in a traffic crash.

Drowsy Driving

As a driver, your number one responsibility is to get yourself and your passengers to your destination safely. When behind the wheel, you always need to be alert and focused. At 55 mph, a vehicle travels the length of a football field in 3.7 seconds. This is no time for a "mini" snooze. Being an attentive driver, and looking out for the driver who isn't, is increasingly important. Drive focused. Stay safe.

Safety Facts for the Road
- Drowsy driving causes more than 100,000 crashes each year, resulting in 40,000 injuries and 1,550 deaths.
- Crashes caused by drowsy driving are often serious crashes and occur most often on high-speed rural highways when the driver is alone.
- Drowsy driving can happen to anyone. A recent National Sleep Foundation study revealed that one half (51%) of adults have driven while drowsy and 17% report having fallen asleep while driving within the past year.

Drive Focused. Stay Safe. Avoid Aggressive Driving.
- Be aware of your behavior and the behavior of others on the road during the late night, early morning and mid-afternoon hours when drowsy driving crashes are most likely to occur. Plan a rest stop during these hours.
- Get a full night of rest before driving. If you become tired while driving, stop. A short nap (15 to 45 minutes) and consuming caffeine can help temporarily.
- Stop at regular intervals when driving long distances. Get out of the car every 2 hours to stretch and walk briskly.
- Set a realistic goal for the number of miles you can safely drive each day.
- Avoid taking medications that cause drowsiness.

Do you know when you're driving drowsy?

Some warning signs of fatigue:
- You can't remember the last few miles driven.
- You hit a rumble strip or drift from your lane.
- Your thoughts are wandering and disconnected.
- You yawn repeatedly.
- You have difficulty focusing or keeping your eyes open.
- You tailgate or miss traffic signs.
- You have trouble keeping your head up.
- You keep pulling your vehicle back into the lane.

If you're tired and are in danger of falling asleep, then you cannot predict when a "mini" sleep may occur. A driver cannot react to road dangers when tired. Getting enough sleep will not only help you feel better, it can save your life.

For more information on aggressive driving, contact NETS at 1-888-221-0045 or visit: www.trafficsafety.org.

On our congested roadways, it's more important than ever to drive with a clear head and a sharp focus. Make it a life-governing rule not to drive when you've had too much to drink. On average, a driver makes over 200 decisions per mile, so it's critical that a driver make the decision to drive alert before getting behind the wheel. Not only will you be a safer driver but you will be in a much better position to defend yourself from the driver who doesn't make that choice. Drive focused. Stay safe.

Safety Facts for the Road

- Alcohol impaired driving accounts for about 40% of fatal crashes.
- About three in every 10 Americans will be involved in an alcohol-related crash at some time in their lives.
- Research shows that alcohol is a contributing factor in 39% of all work-related traffic crashes.
- Nearly 1.5 million people are arrested each year for driving while intoxicated (DWI). Two-thirds of all drivers arrested for DWI are first time offenders.
- A DWI/DUI conviction on a person's driving record may prevent them from getting a job, receiving a promotion or even result in a job loss.
- Many companies have corrective action programs that suspend company driving privileges for a DWI/DUI violation.
- Nine out of 10 insurance companies automatically cancel the policy of a driver convicted of a DWI/DUI violation. Consequently, the driver must find a high-risk insurance company and face substantial rate increases.

Drive Focused. Stay Safe. Avoid Aggressive Driving.

- Alcohol involvement is highest at night (9 p.m. to 6 a.m.), on weekends and on holidays.
- Driving skills, especially judgment, are impaired in most people long before they exhibit visible signs of drunkenness.
- Celebrations are a part of our lives and sometimes they include alcohol. They should not, however, involve impaired driving:
  - Decide who is the designated driver before the party starts.
  - Be the kind of co-worker who will take the keys if someone has had too much to drink.
  - If you're impaired, make the safe choice – ride with a designated driver, call a taxi, stay where you are, or call a sober friend or family member. Making the safe choice could save your life.

Can you spot an impaired driver on the road?

Drivers under the influence of alcohol often display certain characteristic driving behaviors. Keep these in mind to avoid a dangerous situation.

- Weaving, swerving, drifting or stradling the center line.
- Driving on the wrong side of the road.
- Driving at a very slow speed.
- Stopping without cause or braking erratically.
- Turning abruptly or responding slowly to traffic signals.
- Driving with the window down in cold weather.
- Driving with headlights off at night.

If you spot an impaired driver, stay a safe distance from their vehicle. Alert the police that there is an unsafe driver on the road.

For more information on aggressive driving, contact NETS at 1-888-221-0045 or visit: www.trafficsafety.org.

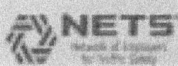 **NETS** Remember, the best defense against aggressive drivers is a seat belt! Buckling up is the single most effective action you can take to protect yourself from serious injury in a traffic crash.

Costs of Motor Vehicle Crashes to Employers Worksheet

Direct Costs to the Organization

Workers' compensation benefits	$
Healthcare costs	$
Increases in medical insurance premiums	$
Auto insurance and liability claims and settlements	$
Physical and vocational rehabilitation costs	$
Life insurance and survivor benefits	$
Group health insurance dependent coverage	$
Property damage (equipment, products, etc.)	$
Motor vehicle repair and replacement	$
EMS costs (ambulance or medivac helicopter)	$
Vehicle towing, impoundment and inspection fees	$
Municipality or utility fees for damage to roads, signs or poles	$

Direct Total $

Indirect Costs

Supervisor's time (rescheduling, making special arrangements)	$
Fleet manager's time to coordinate vehicle repair, replacement, etc.	$
Reassignment of personnel to cover for missing employees (less efficient)	$
Overtime pay (to cover work of missing employees)	$
Employee replacement	$
Re-entry and retraining of injured employees	$
Administrative costs (documentation of injuries, treatment, absences, crash investigation)	$
Inspection costs	$
Failure to meet customer requirements resulting in loss of business	$
Bad publicity, loss of business	$

Indirect Total $

TOTAL $

32

www.ingramcontent.com/pod-product-compliance
Lightning Source LLC
Chambersburg PA
CBHW081755170526
45167CB00009B/4035